TRADITIONAL NOTES

To Marj.
For your constant love, support and belief in me.
Who would have thought?

TRADITIONAL NOTES
A Celebration of Irish Music and Musicians

Photography and Text by
Stephen Power

The Liffey Press

Published by
The Liffey Press
Ashbrook House, 10 Main Street
Raheny, Dublin 5, Ireland
www.theliffeypress.com

© 2011 Stephen Power

A catalogue record of this book is
available from the British Library.

ISBN 978-1-908308-01-6

Printed in Spain by GraphyCems.

Contents

Acknowledgements

A Note of Thanks

I am indebted to all of the musicians and instrument makers featured in this book who gave up their time to allow me to photograph them. Many of them welcomed me into their homes and workshops or allowed me to attend concerts and interrupt sound checks. Without their assistance and cooperation this book would not have happened.

Making contact with key people was a primary challenge and several people were instrumental in making that happen. Clare fiddler Denis Liddy was extremely helpful, and by offering access to his extensive list

of contacts he assisted me in getting the work started. Similarly, Ennis bouzouki player Eoin O'Neill also gave generous access to his contact book in the early stages of the work.

During the course of the photography, a number of musicians and instrument makers freely offered their invaluable advice that has helped shape the overall look of the book. In particular, I am especially grateful to Paddy Clancy, Kevin Crawford and Noel Hill for their support and assistance to my project.

Two bands and certain musicians feature prominently in the book, and I am especially grateful to them for their patience and extra-special help. Namely, they are: Lúnasa (Sean Smyth, Cillian Vallely, Kevin Crawford, Paul Meehan and Trevor Hutchinson) and De Dannan (Alec Finn, Johnny 'Ringo' McDonagh, Derek Hickey, Brian McGrath, Mick Conneely, Eleanor Shanley, Cian Finn and their manager Pearse Doherty).

My friends John Meighan and Gerry Fitzgibbon provided some of the instruments that I photographed in my studio, including Gerry's own impressive collection of uilleann pipes, whistles, guitar and bodhrán and his partner Ber's Ruddall Rose flute. Gerry is also included in some of the shots in the uilleann pipes chapter.

The team at West Cork Music offered access to sound checks for the Masters of Tradition concerts in Bantry, West Cork.

Carsten Panduro, artistic director of the Toender Folk Festival in Denmark, was very generous in offering a photography pass to all areas of the festival and also providing transport from Hamburg airport and arranging hotel accommodation.

Tracy Crawford of Bally-O Promotions, in County Clare, warrants a special mention – and a very big 'thank you' – for her tremendous help and support for the book, including offering to arrange contact with a number of musicians, which helped resolve many logistical issues.

Professor Mícheál Ó Súilleabháin of the Irish World Academy of Music and Dance at the University of Limerick has supported the project in a number of important ways and I am extremely grateful to him and other members of the academy staff including Ellen Byrne, Press and Performing Arts Coordinator, for their invaluable assistance.

Every book needs a good publisher and I feel particularly fortunate that I found David Givens of The Liffey Press for this one. David saw the potential in this book after reading the proposal and gave me the green light at our first meeting. His calm encouragement and impressive editorial skills have helped produce a book of which I can be proud.

Marjorie Brickley has been a constant source of encouragement throughout this entire project. Without a word of complaint she has accompanied me on many of the physical journeys I made – and all of the emotional ones. Although it may sound like a cliché to say that this book is unlikely to have happened without her – it is certainly how I genuinely feel and I can't thank her enough.

Foreword

There is a famous conundrum: what is an occasional table when it's not being a table? Perhaps you could also ask: what is a musical instrument when it is not being played? When it is snug in its box at night, or tucked under an arm on the bus, does it have a life? Or a memory of all the notes, sounds, tunes and airs that have been coaxed from it over many years, and from many hands? Does it become a small personality, a character, with a unique relationship to the person who plays it, and who looks after it, cleans it, polishes it and keeps it safe?

Well, maybe . . . but an instrument's prime reason for existence is to make noise, or create sound, if you want to be genteel. To be brought to life in the playing of it. No one spends hundreds of hours finely crafting a fiddle so that it can hang upon the wall. When a master craftsman's skills dovetail into the artistry of a fine musician, it represents a most satisfying synthesis of human expression. The journey from tree in the forest to workbench to musician's hands is long and intricate; at the end, you pick up your instrument to feel it, tune it, test it, breathe its incense . . . and then the magic starts.

It is this magic that Stephen Power captures with these photographs. The meeting of craft and art, the joy and intensity of playing music, the spell cast by fingers deft as a conjurer, are here in close-up. The care, concentration and refinement that yield such beautiful and seductive objects. We are drawn into the visual dimension of an aural art . . . we can see the mischief, delight and depth in the eyes of the performers, and when those eyes are closed, we are drawn in even further.

Put this book up to your ear. See what you can hear.

Ellen Cranitch
Presenter
'Grace Notes'
Lyric FM

Introduction

Introductory Note

Certain things happened in my younger life that, when they came together, led to the creation of this book — over forty years later.

The first thing was that at the age of eleven, and having just started senior school in Merseyside, in the UK, I joined the school brass band. I no longer remember why that happened, or even how it happened, but I do remember that it was a very significant event in my life. During the time spent learning to read music and badly blowing a b-flat cornet, I realised that I had a very strong, perhaps innate, love of music. I also realised, almost simultaneously, that I would never make the grade as a musician. I knew what my lips and fingers were meant to do in order to create a melodious sound — but I just didn't know how to make them do it.

Following the brass band experience, and like many other teenage boys, I progressed to a cheap guitar and learned to play a few chords. I even wrote a few songs – one made my sister cry when I sang it to her – which helped confirm my view that musicians need talent in addition to passion in order to succeed.

The next significant event happened when I was sixteen years old and delivering newspapers early one morning in a leafy suburb in my home town of Prescot. I walked past a house where a man in his mid-thirties was loading camera equipment and a large clear plastic bag full of film into his car. We said 'hello' and – without asking him anything at all – I decided two things instantaneously: One, He was a professional photographer setting off on an assignment (probably for a well-known magazine); and, two, that was how I wanted to spend my entire working life.

To this day, I have no idea if I guessed his occupation correctly. For all I know, he could have been a camera salesman, or a burglar, or something entirely different. But my conviction that I wanted to spend my life as a professional photographer remained strong and has not left me yet.

As with my love of music, I can't really be sure where my passion for photography came from, but come it did, in a big way. I remember being given an old Kodak Box-Brownie to use when I was about eight years old, and from there I became interested in making home-movies on a Super-8 camera for the early part of my teenage years. I went back to stills photography aged nineteen when I bought my first serious SLR camera, a Zenith-E, made in Eastern Europe. At £28, this was a considerable investment for a young man earning around the same amount per month. But, I didn't get very much for my money, other than a solidly built camera body, with a reliable shutter and a pin-sharp lens.

Irish-style bouzouki

John Spillane

Mick Conneely with bouzouki and fiddle

Sean Smyth with fiddle

Unlike today's cameras, there was no auto-focus or built-in exposure metres – and none of the other bells and whistles that often come as standard on modern cameras. And, that was the best thing that could have happened to me – because I had no option other than to teach myself how to focus a camera lens, and how to set an exposure from a held-held light metre and many other essential aspects of photographic technique. Finally, I had found an instrument that I really could play.

Mícheál Ó Súilleabháin's piano, painted by the artist Henry Morgan

The third significant event happened in the early 1980s when I was working as a freelance photographer for a small-circulation magazine aimed at school career advisors. I was contributing a series of features on interesting job opportunities, when I was asked to interview and photograph the new owner of a theatre in Liverpool that had been threatened with demolition. The new boss had decided to instil a new lease of life into the moribund old theatre, by turning it into a venue for rock music. He ripped out the stall seats, and booked some of the top British and American rockers to play. It was a huge success, as was the outcome of my interview, as I was invited to come and photograph (in the orchestra 'pit') as often as I wanted.

It was at the first gig at the Royal Court Theatre, Liverpool that my love of music and my passion for photography came together in a powerful and exciting way. I have photographed many other subjects so far – and I get great enjoyment from them all – but, the thrill I get from standing so close to top-class musicians doing their thing, and being able to photograph them, has never been equalled for me.

I have had an interest in Irish traditional music for many years, both as a listener and a rudimentary player of the bouzouki, plus a four-year experience of owning a traditional music shop (selling musical instruments and traditional music CDs).

However, it is important for me to clarify, from the outset, that this is chiefly a book of photography. Although the subjects are traditional Irish musicians and instrument makers, I make no claim to being an expert or authority on the genre. The written notes are there to supplement the photographs, but they are not offered as a comprehensive guide to traditional Irish music. Most of the information included in the notes has been gleaned either from the artists directly or via official sources. That said, any errors are entirely my own.

Alec Finn's bouzouki

I have included some anecdotal notes, which I hope will give an insight into my personal experiences of meeting and photographing these interesting and talented people.

My goal for this book was to provide a photographic *celebration* of traditional Irish musicians and instrument makers living and working in Ireland. The book is arranged, by alphabetical order, into chapters focusing on some of the main instruments played by traditional Irish musicians, with sections on some of the musicians who play those instruments and, occasionally, those who make them.

The photography took place in my studio in County Limerick (portraits of the instruments and some musicians) and on location where I photographed instrument makers in their workshops and musicians in their own homes or in places that are special to them, and at performance venues where they were making sound checks and/or playing live concerts.

Some may say that the book is limited in its scope and that it only barely scratches the surface of what is really happening in the traditional Irish music world, today. And they may well be right.

My hope, though, is that you will enjoy getting a glimpse into this fascinating world, which I am able to show you through my camera lens. And, if it makes you want to see – and hear – more, that will definitely be something to celebrate.

Stephen Power
September 2011
Ardagh, County Limerick

1. The Accordion

A Note on the Accordion

The accordion is part of a family referred to as 'free reed' instruments, many of which were developed in the early nineteenth century, and includes the melodeon (an accordion with a single row of keys – or 'buttons' – the two-row button accordion, the piano accordion, the concertina and even the harmonica. The players I have photographed for this section all use the two-row button accordion and I have included some studio shots of a beautiful, and old, Hohner Verdi piano accordion. Incidentally, you won't hear many two-row button players talking about their accordions – the usual term for that instrument is 'the box'.

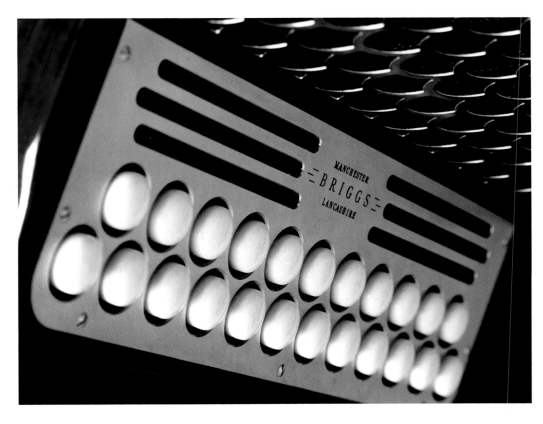

Briggs Accordion
(owned by Derek Hickey)

Briggs Accordion
(owned by Derek Hickey)

A Note on Joe Burke

Joe Burke was born in East Galway in 1939 and gave his first public performance in November 1955. He is widely regarded as a master accordion player who started a huge revival of interest in the instrument. His live performances, as well as his own charm and wit have made him a favourite with all lovers of Irish music. His first recordings (for Gael Linn in the 1950s) were released on 78 rpm discs and were to be the last 78s ever released in Europe. His recording career has spanned five decades and all formats from 78s to CDs. His classic solo albums have sold worldwide and the early ones are considered collec-

This living legend of Irish traditional music – who didn't know me at all when I called him – invited us into his home, showed us his hilarious collection of humorous posters designed by Joe to advertise the monthly trad sessions at his local pub, asked his dog Patsy to play the piano for us (below is photographic evidence of this) and even offered us cheese and wine late into the evening. This is one photo shoot I won't forget in a hurry.

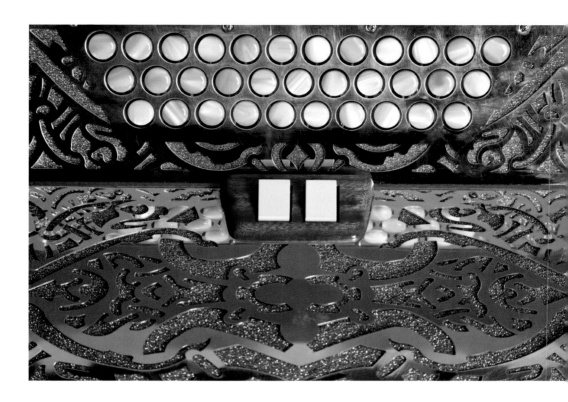

A Note on Paddy Clancy – Accordion Maker

Paddy Clancy was born in 1965 into a house steeped in the Irish music tradition. His father, Paddy Snr., who also plays the box, instilled a passion in his son for the instrument and its possibilities.

A promising career in traditional Irish music began at the age of fourteen with the award of young musician of the year in 1979. Further accolades were soon to follow with Munster senior competition titles in 1986, 1987 and 1988; also in 1988 Paddy was crowned All Ireland senior accordion champion at the Fleadh Ceol in Kilkenny at the age of twenty-three. This prestigious award provided Paddy with the opportunity to forge strong friendships and to travel on the Comhaltas tour of the USA and Canada in 1989.

Paddy's love of music didn't stop there, as an interest in accordion construction and design led him to a career in accordion manufacturing and repair. Paddy then established his own personal accordion range which he is proud to give the family name to. The business is located at his family home in Ballingarry, County Limerick.

*Paddy Clancy in his workshop (above), the tools of the trade (bottom left)
and trying out the finished article (bottom right)*

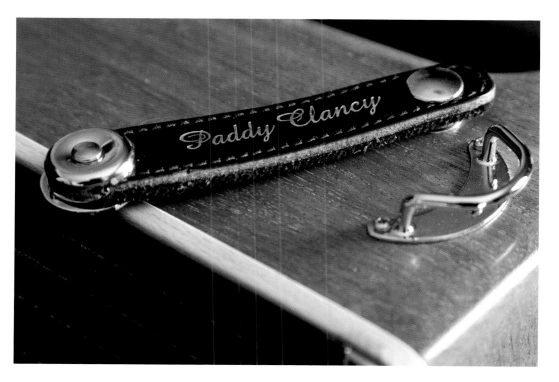

Viewing room in Paddy Clancy's workshop

A Note on Derek Hickey

I've known Derek Hickey since I moved to his home town of Adare in County Limerick, in 1999. This quiet, unassuming, humorous and extremely talented box player is one of the most likeable musicians on the traditional music circuit. He has played as a member of the band Arcady and with many notable Irish musicians including Frankie Gavin and with Alec Finn and Johnny McDonagh in De Dannan.

A Note on Séamus Begley

Accordion player and singer Séamus Begley, from West County Kerry, is the quintessential Irish musician, an eager storyteller known for his sharp wit and famous for pumping out tune after tune at all night sessions. His repertoire reflects his own place and his style of playing is much influenced by a now gone generation of accordion and fiddle players who came to céilí in his family home. Séamus's style is unique and he is considered by many to be one of the finest players of the dance music of West Kerry and is never happier than when people are dancing to his music. Séamus divides his time between his small holding in the West Kerry Gaeltacht and travelling Ireland and the world playing music. He has toured extensively with Jim Murray, Altan, Steve Cooney and Mary Black to name but a few (from seamusbegleyandjimmurray.ie).

Hohner Verdi Piano Accordion

A Note on Charlie Harris

Charlie Harris, TG4's Traditional Irish Musician of the Year in 2009, was born in Kilmallock, County Limerick, and was inspired by the playing of the late Joe Cooley, amongst others. He is also well known for his early recordings with the group Shaskeen. I found Charlie to be a quietly spoken, extremely polite and gentle giant of a man who is widely respected for his musicianship and highly regarded as a supreme stalwart of traditional music.

2. The Banjo

A Note on the Banjo

The banjo has its roots in African folk music, and the five-string version (including a shorter 'drone-string') has become a popular instrument playing Old-Time and Bluegrass music. The tenor banjo, which has four strings and a shorter neck, is typically (but not exclusively) the instrument used for traditional Irish music. It is often tuned to GDAE – as is a fiddle – and so it is not unusual to find that good Irish traditional banjo players can also play the fiddle well, and vice-versa.

A Note on Brian McGrath

Brian McGrath comes from Brookeborough, County Fermanagh, in Northern Ireland. He started playing piano at age five and later progressed to the accordion and then the banjo and mandolin, and has won a number of All-Ireland titles on these instruments.

Brian's first work in the professional field was with the group Dervish playing banjo and mandolin. He then joined Four Men and a Dog and played on the award-winning album *Barking Mad*, featuring again on banjo and mandolin. He then moved his career on with some accompaniment work with Noel Hill, Paul Brock and Frankie Gavin, to name a few, before joining the Sean Keane Band as pianist. After seven successful years Brian joined the super-group De Dannan where he remains as a stalwart member, playing banjo and piano.

A Note on Barney McKenna

Barney McKenna was born in the Donnycarney area of Dublin in 1939, became interested in music at the age of six and is considered by many to be one of the world's greatest banjo players. He spent a few months playing with The Chieftains before becoming a founder member of The Dubliners in 1962.

Folk music historian and fellow banjoist Mick Moloney has said that Barney McKenna is single-handedly responsible for making the GDAE tuned tenor banjo the standard banjo in Irish music.

During one of the shoots for this book, I found myself outlining the list of yet-to-shoot-subjects to the well-known accordion maker Paddy Clancy. When I got to 'banjo' I sensed an increased note of seriousness in Paddy's tone of voice, as he told me: 'Look, there's really no point in having a section on the banjo if you're not going to photograph Barney McKenna.' It was a fairly worrying statement, as even with the best will in the world I could not see how that might happen. I didn't know Barney McKenna and I didn't know how to make contact with him. I put the idea on the back burner, feeling that although Paddy had a point, it seemed unlikely that I could achieve that particular photographic goal.

On the last weekend before I was planning to stop photographing and start work on the post-processing, Marj and I flew to the Toender folk festival in Denmark to photograph some traditional Irish bands playing live – particularly De Dannan and Lúnasa. On the Sunday after a long and tiring day's photography – which wasn't made any easier by torrential rain, and the fact that the rubber boot shops were closed – we made our

way back to the hotel, wondering if we would dry our shoes off in time to venture out for the final show of the festival, while trying to remember who was playing. We said hello to a woman standing in the hotel doorway and started to chat about the weather and the festival in general. I'm not sure what question it was that Marj asked, but the answer that the lady gave included the phrase, 'I've known Barney for twenty years'. The light bulb in my damp brain flickered and I knew exactly who was playing the headline concert that night: The Dubliners. We dried off, changed and went to find dinner. Then, on my very last scheduled day of shooting, I did what Paddy Clancy had encouraged me to do a few months previously. I photographed Barney McKenna playing the banjo. It's funny how, sometimes, the things that are meant to happen, happen – even when it seems extremely unlikely that they will.

Quentin Cooper

Clare musician Quentin Cooper playing his Framus banjo at the Glor theatre in Ennis. (See the Bouzouki, Guitar and Mandolin chapter for a note on Quentin Cooper.)

A Note on Patsy Watchorn

A real Dubliner in every sense of the word, Patsy Watchorn – of The Dubliners – came from a very musical family and there was always music in the house. In the late 1960s, Patsy gained his first experiences of performing live with a band named The Quare Fellas. After two albums, Patsy left the group to pursue new directions.

The early 1970s saw him rehearsing in his own home with Mick Crotty and soon they formed a new group, the Dublin City Ramblers. In 1995, Patsy decided it was time to change gears again and left the Ramblers to pursue his solo career.

Patsy joined The Dubliners in 2005 singing and playing the banjo, bodhrán and spoons. He cites Luke Kelly, former lead singer with The Dubliners, as his favourite singer.

I was fortunate enough to photograph Patsy – with his distinctive Deering 'Black Diamond' banjo – when The Dubliners headlined the 2011 Toender folk festival in Denmark. I then enjoyed a very entertaining trip in the company of Patsy and other musicians travelling home.

3. The Bodhrán and Bones

A Note on the Bodhrán

The bodhrán (pronounced 'bow-rawn', rhyming 'bow' with 'cow') is an ancient Irish drum, traditionally made from cured goatskin stretched over a circular wooden frame, which can be any size from eight inches to twenty-four inches in diameter. The smaller drums are often painted with Celtic symbols and used for decoration – but those intended for serious playing have undecorated skins and are usually fourteen to eighteen inches in diameter. Some bodhráns (called 'tune-able') have a system of screws inside the rim which allow the skin to be tightened or slacked which, in effect, alters the pitch allowing them to be 'tuned'.

Some say the Irish word *bodhrán* translates to 'skin tray', which would fit with the idea that it may have started life as method of carrying cut turf from the bog, and later – with holes cut in the skin – as a sieve for sifting wheat from chaff. The writer John B. Keane is reported to have said that because it replaced the tambourine in Irish music, the name came from a corruption of that name – tambourine to 'bourine' to bodhrán. Others think the name might derive from the Irish word *bodhor*, which refers to a 'soft' or 'dull' sound. Intriguingly, there are those who say it might refer to the Irish word *bodhar*, meaning 'deaf' or 'haunting', but that might just be mischievousness. However, those who asked the famous Irish piper Seamus Ennis for his advice on the proper way to play the bodhrán are likely to have been told, 'with an open penknife'. Now, that is mischievous.

A Note on Johnny 'Ringo' McDonagh

Johnny 'Ringo' McDonagh, from County Galway, has been playing the bodhrán since 1967 and was a founder member of De Dannan, together with Alec Finn and Frankie Gavin. He subsequently left to form his own successful band Arcady before re-joining De Dannan in recent years. Also an expert bones player, Johnny has toured Europe with Mike Oldfield – and features on the first live recording of *Tubular Bells* – and has recorded with many other artists including Altan, Eileen Ivers, Mary Bergin and even Phil Lynott (of Thin Lizzy).

Fellow bodhrán maestro Tommy Hayes cites Johnny McDonagh as 'the finest traditional player', although McDonagh's natural modesty probably means he doesn't take the praise too seriously. Many would, though.

Had I known as much about Johnny 'Ringo' McDonagh's Irish music credentials as I've gathered since first speaking to him, I might have been totally overawed and unable to string a coherent sentence together. But maybe not, as I found myself talking easily with a very softly spoken, friendly and unassuming man who, during the time I was travelling with and photographing him, was extremely helpful and supportive of my work.

One particularly notable moment was during the sound check for a De Dannan concert in Denmark. I was at the edge of the stage talking to the MC for the show, who was explaining that there would be no designated area for photographers at the show itself, so I would have to arrange to be at the venue just ahead of the crowd (and the large auditorium was sold out) to jostle for a vantage point. The discussion had been going on for a few minutes when Johnny left his seat on the stage, knelt down right in front of me and asked, 'Are you OK? Is there a problem?' I explained the situation and Johnny replied, 'OK good, I was worried that you were being told not to take photographs' and went back to his seat, reassured. Shortly afterwards the MC (also a genuinely helpful man) invited Marj and me to have dinner in the private dining room for the bands and crew, which would enable us to get back into the concert hall ahead of the audience and find a good seat from which to photograph the show. I somehow felt Johnny's quiet and helpful influence on that offer, too.

A Note on Tommy Hayes

I first met Tommy Hayes when I owned an Irish music shop in the village of Adare in County Limerick in 2002. One afternoon, I watched a man carefully examine some of the tuneable bodhráns I had displayed in a rack, by very carefully 'pinging' them with his fingers and holding his ear close to the skin as he did so. While he was testing the drums, I was opening a copy of the CD *A Room in the North* and scrutinising the photograph on the sleeve, to make sure that I was right about my hunch that a major Irish musician had walked into my small shop.

I introduced myself to this affable man — known in the Adare area as 'Tommy Spoons' — and got into a conversation that led to Tommy giving

a very well-received bodhrán class a few weeks later, which was attended by (amongst others) the editor of *Irish Music* magazine, an American tourist on vacation who re-arranged his travel plans to attend the workshop, and an enthusiast from the UK who flew over especially for the pleasure of a two-hour tutorial from this well-respected, ever-smiling, legend of the Irish drum world.

Tommy Hayes is originally from Kildimo in County Limerick and now lives in Feakle, County Clare. He was a member of Stockton's Wing from the band's inception in 1977 to 1983, recording four seminal albums. He was the original percussionist for Riverdance and performed with the shows in Dublin, London, Washington DC and Belfast.

He has released two solo albums, *An Ras* and *A Room in the North,* being the first Irish percussionist to do so. Music from both albums has been used in a variety of television and independent media productions.

Tommy has recorded with many artists, and to date has recorded output numbers in excess of 400 albums. Tommy has played on numerous films amongst them *Titanic, The Devil's Own, Rob Roy, In the Name of the Father* and *The Field.* Tommy is also very involved in teaching and has held workshops and master classes in many parts of the globe.

Tommy returned to college in 2000 and received a Masters Degree from the University of Limerick in Music Therapy. He currently works in a variety of clinical placements, while actively pursuing his career in music (source: www.hayesleslie.com).

A Note on a Bodhrán Maker, Malachy Kearns

In Roundstone, Connemara, County Galway I discovered that there is a tradition of giving certain locals a nickname that best fits what they look like or what they do, probably just as a way of making them more easily identifiable. Because of that tradition, once you've made initial contact, you're more likely to get a text message or email (often ending in 'soup is ready and waiting for you') not from Malachy Kearns but Malachy Bodhrán.

He is a large, affable man who seems to have a huge appetite for life and has become one of the best known bodhrán makers in Ireland. Malachy started making bodhráns in 1976, training with Peadar Mercier of The Chieftains, and made the bodhráns for Riverdance, and Christy Moore uses his drums – and the testimony from him, 'I kneel in prayer towards Roundstone' adorns a large photograph of the musician in Kearns' large and always well-populated craft shop, where you can buy anything from a small hand-painted ornamental bodhrán to a full-sized professional standard instrument.

A Note on John-Jo Kelly

John-Jo Kelly is an extraordinarily talented younger generation bodhrán player from Manchester, UK. He has played with a number of top traditional music artists, including the band Altan and Paul Brady and his own band, Flook. I photographed him at the World Fleadh in Ballybunnion, County Kerry, in 2006.

A Note on Ger Hoyne

Ger Hoyne, who is the best dressed bodhrán player I have yet to meet, is from Ennis, County Clare and has been playing the bodhrán since he was eighteen. He became interested in Irish music because his father is a banjo player – an instrument Ger is also learning. He plays with the Clare band The Céilí Bandits and also in Sunday sessions at Brogan's Bar in Ennis. 'The sound of the bodhrán resonates with me,' Ger told me.

Lecturer Sandra Joyce playing the bodhrán and below with Dónal Lunny and John Carty

A Note on the Bones

The bones, as used as a musical instrument, pre-date Irish music by a very long time. American bones expert Scott C. Miller told me that there is evidence of bones being used for both musical and ceremonial purposes in both ancient China and ancient Egypt dating back to 3300 BC.

Despite the name, the instrument is often made of shaped wood, although some players prefer the traditional animal bones – usually beef ribs as shown on the previous page. Connoisseurs will have a number of sets in their collection of varying shapes and materials, each producing their own unique sound. They are typically about five to seven inches long and gently curved. To play the bones, you hold at least two (some players can use four in one hand) between your fingers, keeping one steady and moving the wrist so that they knock against each other. I watched the great Yirdy Machar giving a bones lesson recently, and I have decided that becoming a renowned concert pianist, even at my advanced years and without being abe to play a note on the piano, would be simpler.

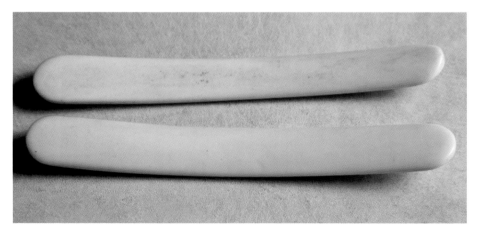

Shaped polished bones

A Note on Yirdy Machar, Bones Player

Yirdy Machar is an award-winning bones player who was born in Scotland and now lives in a wooden cottage under a large oak tree at the edge of a forest on the island of Sealland in Denmark. His passions include singing, playing music, giving workshops on bones and bodhrán, and teaching the fine art of calligraphy. Yirdy has performed with many bands and although his main love is bones, he also plays the bodhrán, spoons, 'a few tunes on the melodeon' (button-box accordion), and tin whistle. In 2002 he won first place in the National Traditional Country Music Association (NTCMA) Bones and Spoons contest. It was here that Yirdy adopted the name 'MacBones' in homage to his late father, who was affectionately known as 'Big Mac'.

*Johnny 'Ringo' McDonnagh of De Dannan discussing bones
with top player Yirdy Machar*

*Yirdy Machar giving a lesson on playing the bones to Marj while
Alec Finn (De Dannan) looks on*

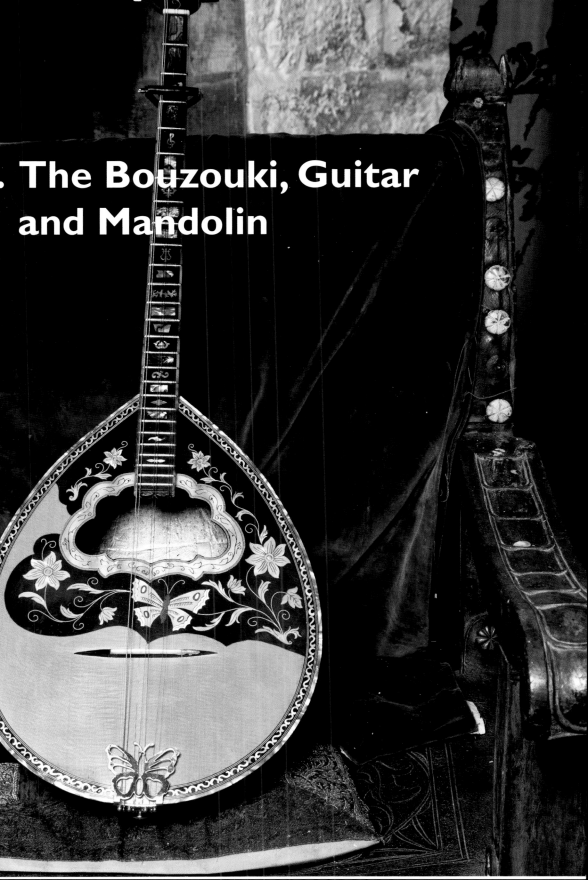

The Bouzouki, Guitar
and Mandolin

A Note on the Bouzouki, Guitar and Mandolin

The bouzouki was first introduced to Irish music by Johnny Moynihan in the 1960s, and at that time only the Greek-style instrument, with six strings – in three pairs, and a bowl back – was available. It later changed shape, gaining a wider, deeper body, and a fourth 'course' (pair) of strings – making it suitable for strumming as well as for melody and counterpoint work. Virtuoso players such as Andy Irvine, Dónal Lunny and Alec Finn have pioneered the use of the instrument in Irish music. Some, such as Finn, have continued to use the Greek-style instrument, while others have adopted the Irish-style bouzouki as their instrument of choice.

There are those who think that the guitar is only used in Irish music for strumming out a reel or jig rhythm, but if so they have never heard it in the hands of Dennis Cahill, Dónal Lunny or Paul Meehan, amongst others. In the right hands, it can produce wonderfully subtle and beautiful music.

The mandolin is, to my mind, the bouzouki's baby brother, often tuned in the same way as a fiddle and probably more suited to playing melodies than its big brother. Its high-pitched tones can soar high above a session, and put the icing on the musical cake.

A Note on Alec Finn

Alec Finn, who was born in Yorkshire, England, started playing the bouzouki by mistake. 'A friend of mine was going to Greece and I asked him to bring me back a lute,' he told me. 'He brought me back a bouzouki by mistake and I started to play around with that. If he'd gone down a different street I'd probably still be playing the guitar and my music would've gone in a whole different direction.'

It's not every day that I'm invited to 'come to the castle and take some photographs', but that was the case when I contacted Alec Finn, bouzouki player extraordinaire and founder-member of legendary Irish traditional band De Dannan. The castle, Alec's home for many years, is situated in Oranmore, County Galway, and I can't think of a more fitting location to photograph one of the all-time great names in Irish traditional music.

A Note on Eoin O'Neill

The well known bouzouki player and teacher Eoin O'Neill was born in Dublin and now lives in County Clare, where is he is a stalwart of the traditional Irish music scene. Eoin plays regular sessions with The Céilí Bandits and a variety of other top Clare players around Ennis and other towns in the Clare area. Eoin was the first musician that I photographed for this book, and even though I did not know him when I first made contact, he has been instrumental (pun intended) in helping me find some of the other players. It is obvious to me that he is a player who is very well regarded and liked by his fellow musicians and traditional Irish music fans worldwide.

A Note on Mick Conneely

The very likeable bouzouki and fiddle player Mick Conneely was born in Bedford, England, of Irish parents. His father Mick comes from Errislannan, near Clifden, County Galway, and his mother Lizzi came from near Newton Forbes, County Longford. Mick senior is known as a fine traditional fiddle player as was his father before him, Máirtín. The Conneely home in Bedford was always full of great music and this environment helped shape Mick's early musical sensibilities. Like many a London-area Irish musician, Mick began formal lessons in Irish music at the age of eleven with the legendary Clare musician and teacher, Brendan Mulkere. Mick has played bouzouki with many well-known traditional musicians, including flute player Kevin Crawford and fiddler Tony Linnane, and plays fiddle in Alec Finn and Johnny McDonagh's re-formed De Dannan.

A Note on Dónal Lunny

Dónal Lunny was born in Tullamore, County Offaly and brought up in Newbridge, County Kildare. Through his work with Planxty, The Bothy Band, Moving Hearts, and as co-founder and producer with Mulligan Records, plus many other numerous achievements, he is regarded as one of the most influential and important figures in Irish music today. Lunny is considered to have had some input into the shape of the Irish-style bouzouki by ordering an instrument with a flat back from luthier Peter Abnett (from England), partly because it made it more comfortable to play.

I have been a fan of Dónal Lunny's music for many years, and found myself being fortunate to tell him so during a photo shoot at a sound check for the Blas summer school concert in Limerick. The real difficulty for me – being in the presence of a true musical genius – was in keeping the camera steady enough to take a sharp photograph!

A Note on Dennis Cahill

Dennis Cahill was born in Chicago to Irish parents and studied at the Chicago Music College. He has performed with such renowned fiddlers as Liz Carroll, Eileen Ivers and Kevin Burke, as well as many Irish musicians on both sides of the Atlantic. He is a sought after producer for musical artists whom he records in his own Chicago studio. But it is for his work with Clare fiddler Martin Hayes that Dennis Cahill is probably best known. I have been privileged to be standing only a few feet away from this outstanding guitarist, while taking photographs, and have sometimes forgotten to press the shutter because I was busy wondering how one man can make a guitar sound like there are four people playing it. Plus – and this is really annoying – Dennis Cahill is also an excellent photographer.

A Note on Paul Meehan

Paul Meehan – guitarist and banjo player with Lúnasa – was born in Manchester and grew up in Armagh. He was a member of the bands Buille and North Cregg and a founder member of the group Na Dorsa with whom he recorded the much acclaimed *The Wild Music of the Gaels*. Paul later joined the Karan Casey band and recorded on two albums, *Distant Shore* and *Chasing the Sun*. He has performed with Altan, At the Racket, Liz Carroll, The Michael McGoldrick Trio, Tommy Peoples, Tededor, The Alan Kelly band and Paddy Keenan.

I met Paul Meehan over dinner, in the private dining room for bands and crew at the Toender Folk festival in Demark. At that point, I already knew that his driving, catchy guitar riffs and rhythms were the backbone of the mighty Lúnasa. I just didn't know what a quietly spoken, extremely friendy person he was, but I do now.

A Note On Eamonn Campbell

Eamonn Campbell, guitarist and singer with The Dubliners since 1987, was born in Drogheda, County Louth, and began playing professionally in 1965 with Dermot O'Brien and The Clubmen. In 1972, he became a studio musician and also played in theatre orchestras, including for *Jesus Christ Superstar, West Side Story* and *Joseph and his Amazing Technicolour Dreamcoat.* He has performed on numerous occasions with the RTÉ concert orchestra, playing guitar, mandolin and banjo.

Eamonn is also considered by many to be one of Ireland's most successful record producers, having produced hits for Paddy Reilly, Foster and Allen, Brendan Grace, Philomena Begley and even American country singer Billy Jo Spears. In 1987, the year he joined The Dubliners as a musician, Eamonn produced The Dubliners' *25 Years Celebration* album and their hit single 'The Irish Rover' recorded with The Pogues.

A Note on Quentin Cooper

Luthier Quentin Cooper has Peruvian and Irish parents, was born in Peru and came to Wicklow at the age of eleven. He is now settled in County Clare and is a regular on the session scene, playing almost nightly with other well-known Clare musicians, such as Eoin O'Neill and Yvonne Casey, in their band The Cieli Bandits and in other session line-ups. He is best known for his playing of the banjo and the fiddle, and he made the mandolin seen here in his workshop in Ennistymon, County Clare.

5. The Concertina

A Note on the Concertina

The concertina is a small, six-sided portable accordion, which comes in two forms: the 'English' type, developed by Sir Charles Wheatstone in 1829 and improved in 1844, and the 'Anglo' type, which is most popular for playing Irish traditional music and was developed in Germany by Carl Freidrich Uhlig in 1834. In Ireland, there is a stronghold of concertina playing in County Clare and it is especially popular amongst women, although one of the most notable players in the world is a man.

A Note on Noel Hill

World renowned concertina player Noel Hill, winner of the 2011 Gradam Ceol (Irish Musician of the Year) from Irish TV channel TG4, was born in County Clare and now lives in the Gaeltacht (Irish-speaking) area of Connemara, County Galway. Noel is widely regarded as one of the major figures in Irish music and, according to *Irish Music Magazine*, his concerts and recordings have developed the concertina to a new level and broadened its appeal to a new audience. He is widely regarded as the foremost concertina player of his generation, and has inspired and taught many young players. He has recorded with artists such as Christy Moore, Paul Brady, Mick Hanly and Mairead Ni Dhomhnaill.

'If you're going to do this book at all, you need to have the very best people you can get in it.' I was sitting, with my partner, Marj, in Noel Hill's kitchen as he told me this while he wrote down contact information for some of the central figures in Irish music today. We'd only just met Noel, but it felt as if we had known him for many years. We were introduced to his children and invited to explore his comfortable home – which boasts the most wonderful view over Galway Bay – for the most suitable location for the photographs. Noel had also laid out his spectacular and probably priceless collection of rare antique accordions on the table. He made us lunch and we enjoyed a memorable few hours in his company. But it didn't stop there. Noel has been instrumental (again, pun intended) in helping me make contact with other Irish music greats, and his encouragement for my project has been enormous. I feel privileged to have met this generous stalwart of the traditional music world.

Aisling Hill

A Note on Lorraine Ní Bhriain

Lorraine is a young concertina player from County Clare who is making a big name for herself on the concert circuit and as a music teacher.

A Note from Lorraine Ní Bhriain

grew up in County Clare in a village beside Ennis called Toonagh. In Toonagh National School every child had the opportunity to play tin whistle when they went into first class and were then encouraged to move on to a different instrument. I started on the tin whistle when I was five or six and moved on to the concertina at the age of seven. My grandfather in Miltown Malbay, in County Clare, used to play concertina although I never heard him play. I decided to start playing one of his old two-row concertinas and very shortly afterwards Frank Custy, the principal of Toonagh National School at the time, found me a suitable concertina and showed me where the notes were. I was taught how to play the instrument by Frank Custy, Dymphna O'Sullivan and Noel Hill.'

'I was very influenced by the music of my teachers, the music of local musicians who I played with in pub sessions, and also by musicians, such as Terry Bingham in Doolin, and Tommy Peoples, who was teaching my sister the fiddle. I grew up playing in sessions in towns, such as, Ennis, Miltown Malbay, Lahinch, Doolin and Lisdoonvarna and continued to play regularly in these places until I left Clare in 2011.'

. The Fiddle

A Note on the Fiddle

The fiddle is the mainstay of traditional Irish music. I haven't done a head count, but it is a fairly safe bet to say that there are probably more fiddles played by traditional Irish musicians than any other instrument. Clare fiddler Yvonne Casey told me that one possible reason for this may be because the sound that the fiddle makes is improved when the number of fiddles being played is increased. This may not be the case for some of the other instruments.

Fiddle owned by Yvonne Casey

Violin made by Kuros Torkzadeh

But, how do you tell a fiddle from violin? During his introduction of the members of the band De Dannan, at a concert in Denmark, bodhrán player Johnny McDonagh was talking about fiddle player Mick Conneely, thus: 'Mick is a very versatile player – in that he plays both the fiddle and the violin. Unfortunately, this evening, he has forgotten to bring his violin with him.'

Although there may have been some members of the audience who took Johnny seriously, there's no such confusion between the fiddle and the violin amongst Irish musicians. Irish traditional music is played on a fiddle, even though the fiddler will have bought the instrument from a violin maker. It is, after all, the same thing.

A Note on Martin Hayes

Martin Hayes – originally from County Clare and currently based in the USA – is widely regarded as one of the most extraordinary talents to emerge in the world of Irish traditional music.

He is the recipient of major national and international awards, including the prestigious Gradam Ceoil (Musician of the Year) in 2008 from the Irish language television station TG4; Man of the Year from the American Irish Historical Society; Folk Instrumentalist of the Year from BBC Radio; a National Entertainment Award (the Irish 'Grammy'); six All-Ireland Fiddle Championships – before the age of nineteen; cited by the Irish *Sunday Tribune* as one of the hundred most influential Irish people in the fields of entertainment, politics and sports in the year 2000, as well as being one of the most important musicians to come out of Ireland in the last fifty years.

He is the Artistic Director of the Masters of Tradition Festival held in August each year at Bantry House in West Cork, where Ireland's most distinguished traditional musicians are invited to play in an exquisite chamber music setting.

A Note on Violin Maker Kuros Torkzadeh

Born in Germany, Kuros Torkzadeh moved to Ireland in 1994. A classically trained and enthusiastic musician, he has been crafting and making instruments for the last fifteen years. Kuros studied at the Newark School of Violin Making where he obtained a diploma and the certificate of city and guilds. He then worked in a series of established workshops in England, France and Ireland gaining experience in the field of set-up work, sound adjustments and the general restoration of instruments. At the same time, this gave him the opportunity to acquire his inspiration while carefully studying a variety of fine old instruments.

Now based in Ballinderreen, near Kinvara, County Galway, he operates a workshop, Kuros Violins, specialising in making violins, violas and celli as well as fine restoration and repair.

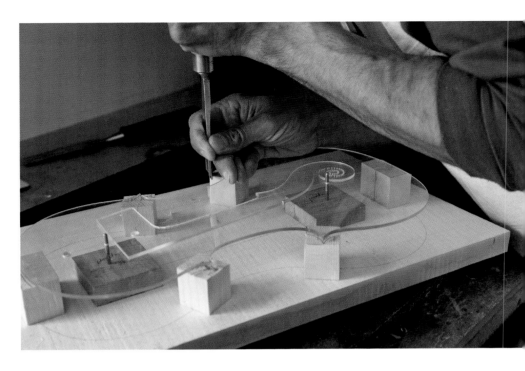

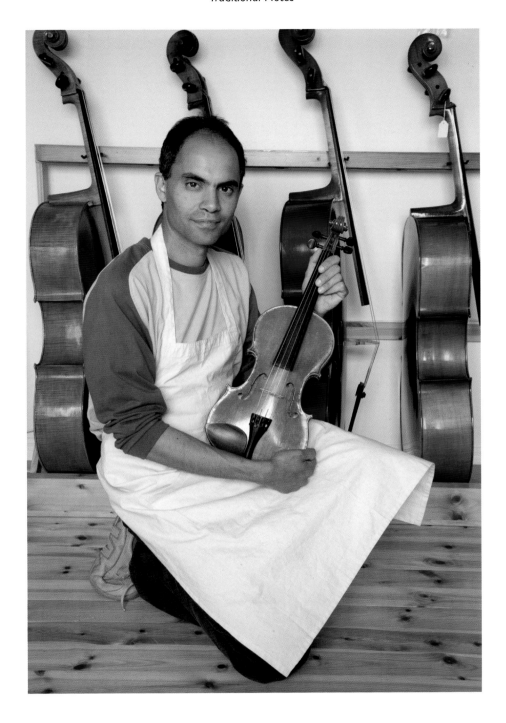

A Note on John Carty

Born in London, and now settled in Boyle, County Roscommon, John Carty has established himself among the elite in Irish traditional music and as a staunch supporter of its preservation. Carty developed his love for the fiddle, banjo, and flute, all of which he has mastered, through his multi-instrumentalist father who was a member of the Glenside Céilí Band in London in the 1960s. At the age of sixteen Carty found himself playing in sessions with some of Irish music's finest and he began to entertain the thought of relocating to Ireland. Carty released his 1994 debut banjo album, *The Cat that Ate the Candle,* to positive reviews. This led to his first fiddle album, *Last Night's Fun,* released on Shanachie Records in 1996. This album has been described as a milestone in recorded fiddle music. In 1997 he formed the band At the Racket, a fun, loose, free-spirited dance band named after an old Flanagan Brothers 78 rpm. The group recorded two highly acclaimed CDs, *At the Racket* and *Mirth Making Heroes,* and toured all the major European festivals.

John Carty was the recipient of the TG4 Gradam Ceoil 'Irish Musician of the Year' in 2003.

A Note on Frankie Gavin

Frankie Gavin was born in 1956 in Corrandulla, County Galway. He comes from a musical family: his father played fiddle as well as his mother and all her family. He started playing the tin whistle at age four, making his first TV appearance three years later. At the age of ten Frankie began to play fiddle and at the age of seventeen he placed first in the All Ireland Fiddle Competition and the All Ireland Flute Competition, both on the same day.

He recorded sixteen albums with De Dannan as well as a number of solo albums, and three collaborations: one a tribute to Joe Cooley entitled *Omos do Joe Cooley* with Paul Brock; a fine collaboration with fellow De Dannan member Alec Finn; and one with Stephane Grapelli exploring the languages of jazz and traditional music. He has also guested with the Rolling Stones on their *Voodoo Lounge* album, with Keith Richards on *Wingless Angels* and with Earl Scruggs, the great US banjo player.

A Note on Yvonne Casey

Yvonne Casey, fiddle player with County Clare group The Céilí Bandits, was encouraged and taught to play the fiddle by influential Toonagh school teacher Frank Custy. Yvonne remembers seeing a fiddle on top of the wardrobe that had been bought in London by her father – it was prob-ably made in China and cost £25 – and when she reached the age of seven she was old enough to reach up for it. 'It was the wood and the strings that really caught my at-tention,' she recalled, 'and

the wonderful sound that I knew it made from listening to recordings of well known players that we had at home.'

A Note on Sean Smyth

Born in Straide, County Mayo, Sean Smyth – the exceptionally talented fiddler with top Irish traditional band Lúnasa – is an All-Ireland champion on both fiddle and whistle. His 1993 solo debut, *The Blue Fiddle*, was named one of the year's ten best albums by *The Irish Echo*. Sean appears on several recordings including *Ceol Tigh Neachtain*, *Music at Matt Molloy's*, Brendan O'Regan's *A Wind of Change*, Alan Kelly's *Out of the Blue* and *Mosaic*, and Dónal Lunny's *Coolfin*.

A Note on Siobhan Peoples

County Clare-based fiddler and fiddle teacher Siobhan Peoples is the daughter of legendary fiddle player Tommy Peoples and the grand-daughter of Kitty Linnane, who played piano with the Kilfenora Céilí Band. A remarkably talented musician, she began playing the fiddle at the age of seven and also cites Frank Custy, the head teacher at her school in Toonagh, as someone who encouraged her to learn the fiddle, probably because both he and her father played the instrument.

7. The Flute

A Note on the Flute

The type of flute mainly used in traditional Irish music is the 'simple-system' flute with a conical-bore. It is usually made of wood, although there are polymer versions available from some makers, which are often seen as cost-effective starter models. The most basic type has six tone holes and no keys, although traditional flutes for more advanced players can be made with up to eight keys fitted. The tone has been described as being more 'airy' and softer than the silver, classical flute found in most orchestras, and it is much smoother and less shrill than the tin whistle.

A Note on Kevin Crawford

Kevin Crawford, originally from Birmingham in the UK and now settled in County Clare, is the flute player and 'chatty man' with the band Lúnasa. Kevin is an extremely talented flute player with a delightful sense of humour and the most welcoming of dispositions – and as such is someone I am sure gains friends and fans wherever he goes. This photographer admits to being in the latter group and hopes that, in time, he makes it to the former.

'How did you become a full-time musician?

'After coming over to Ireland, I was just doing sessions around Clare for the first few years and I thought that was all I really wanted to do – just to be immersed in the tradition and I was happy just to be playing every night in sessions. I had a day job in a music shop in Ennis and then I was picked to host a traditional music radio programme for Clare FM, and I did that for four years. I'd go from working in the music shop, to the radio show, to play in a session all in the same day – so I was involved in music for every waking minute of the day.'

'In October 1996, just after I had married Tracy, I got a phone call from Sean Smyth (fiddle player in Lúnasa) who invited me to go on tour with them in Australia early the following year. I turned him down, at first, as I was newly married and I had started a new job in sales with Clare FM, which I was enjoying. Shortly afterwards, I was out for lunch with the sales manager of Clare FM and was telling him about Sean's offer. He told me that I should go as it would be foolish to turn down such a great opportunity – and that he would cover my work for me while I was away.

So, I went off on a six-week tour with the lads in February 1997, came back and did a number of gigs around Ireland, made a recording, got an invitation to go back to Australia the following year and it was then we decided to give up all our day jobs, and put all our eggs in the one basket. That was fifteen years ago and we haven't looked back.

We've a great team in place and we get on so well as a band, and we're very lucky that we 'clicked', and we still enjoy the work and get massively excited by doing a gig or making a recording.'

A Note on Eamonn Cotter

Eamonn Cotter is a well-known flute player and flute maker from Kilmaley in County Clare. He plays with the traditional group Shaskeen and is widely sought after as a traditional flute maker. I was fortunate enough to meet and photograph Eamonn when he was playing at the Masters of Tradition concerts in Bantry, County Cork.

Frankie Gavin Playing the Flute

Frankie Gavin won first place both in the All Ireland under-18 fiddle and flute competitions, when he was seventeen years old. He released the highly acclaimed flute album *Up and Away* in 1983. I took this photograph of him playing flute at the World Fleadh in Ballybunnion, County Kerry. See 'The Fiddle' chapter for a full note on Frankie Gavin.

Flute students at the Blas summer school

Rudall Rose keyed flute, circa 1850

8. The Harp

A Note on the Harp

The harp can be seen everywhere in Ireland; on coins, pint glasses in pubs, government department headed note paper, the tails of commercial airliners and there is even a large and beautiful one made of plants and flowers on a roundabout close to Limerick city.

The state symbol of Ireland – the harp – is a musical instrument that dates back many centuries and early surviving harps in Ireland date to about the fifteenth century. The Trinity College harp, one of Ireland's national treasures, is the harp from which the national symbol of Ireland is copied. Travelling harpists in Ireland were known to be at the focal point of rebellions – so much so that the harp was banned. Turlough Carolan (1670-1738), the blind Irish folk harpist, wrote hundreds of tunes on the harp and is credited by some with coining, or at least being one of the first to use the term, 'Planxty' (meaning a 'tribute to') in the title of some of his tunes, such as 'Planxty David' and 'Planxty Irwin'.

A Note on a Harper, Michelle Mulcahy

Michelle Mulcahy is one of Ireland's most talented and gifted young multi-instrumentalists. She is a regular performer and tutor worldwide and has toured extensively in Europe, the United States, Canada, China, Australia and Vietnam. Michelle has three highly acclaimed albums recorded by American record label Shanachie and Irish record label Chlo-Iar Chonnachta.

She was awarded the prestigious TG4 Young Musician of the Year in 2006 and Female Musician of the Year in 2005 at the Live-Ireland awards in the United States. She recorded with Bill Whelan and the Irish Chamber Orchestra on the highly acclaimed *Connemara Suite* album.

Michelle completed her Bachelor of Arts degree in Music in University College Cork and progressed on to postgraduate study at the University of Limerick where she graduated with a first class Master's degree in Ethnomusicology and, in the following year, Music Education. She went on to study for her Ph.D in the Irish World Academy of Music at the University of Limerick.

An Interview with Michelle Mulcahy

Who are your main musical influences?

'I have a wide range of influences across the different instruments, including my own father Mick, Noel Hill, Tommy Peoples, Tony MacMahon, Brian Rooney, Joe Cooley, Denis Murphy, Padraig O Keeffe, Patrick Kelly, John Kelly, Seamus Ennis, Willie Clancy, Joe Heaney, Matt Molloy, Tony Linnane, Connie O Connell, Michael Rooney and Laoise Kelly.'

How Important is Irish traditional music to you?

'Irish traditional music is a custodial tradition, which has existed within my family for generations. My childhood, teenage and current adult years all centralize around the art of music making and the art of musical creativity. Music has always been a huge part of my family life and household, a love of music, which has been handed down to me by both my parents. As a performing musician the music itself communicates a private language, a language that is expressive, rich and intensely articulate where the harp is the ultimate voice. My musical upbringing and the value systems and belief transmitted to me by my father are reflected innately within my own creative process as a performing artist.'

Why do you play the Harp ?

'On encountering the sound of the harp aged eight, I was instantly en-
thralled by the beauty of it. It was as if the sound had a spell-binding
effect on me and I was instantly drawn to the powerful acoustics or
draíocht of the harp. The Celtic harp itself represents the mysticism, the
lyrical majesty and beauty of Irish music, song, poetry and language. But
yet it stands for steadfast independence, loyalty, pride and centuries-
long striving and struggle for an Irish identity. Having performed on the
harp itself to audiences worldwide, the concept of affect is paramount
both on the listener, musician and as a performing harpist myself. It is
the harp which I feel personifies the notion of *draíocht* and has a powerful magic that creates an expressive space for a mix of emotions and
passion both for the musician and listener alike.'

Harp contestant at Limerick County Fleadh Ceoil

9. The Piano

A Note on the Piano

There is some debate about whether or not the piano should be listed as a traditional Irish musical instrument, and many 'purists' would argue that it has no place in such a list.

But noted Clare traditional pianist Geraldine Cotter, in her book *Seinn an Piano* (*Play the Piano*), points out that there are references to its use since the eighteenth century, when Edward Bunting published the first edition of *Ancient Music of Ireland* in 1796 and arranged the airs (slow melodies) for the piano. She also says that a later collection of tunes by George Petrie published in 1855 for the Society for the Preservation and Publication of the Melodies of Ireland also contained airs arranged for the piano.

Geraldine goes on to say that recordings of the piano being used to play traditional Irish music were made as far back as the 1920s, often as accompaniment for other instruments, such as the accordion and the fiddle. Around this time, the piano also became a regular feature of Céilí bands, and remains so today – but often in its more portable version of the eletronic piano.

A Note on Mícheál Ó Súilleabháin

Composer and performer Mícheál O Súilleabháin is Chair of Music and Founder/Director of the Irish World Academy of Music and Dance at the University of Limerick.

Noted for his development of a uniquely Irish traditional piano style, he has recorded extensively with the Irish Chamber Orchestra and has released some fifteen recordings overall. He was awarded an Honorary D.Mus from the National University of Ireland at his Alma Mater, University College Cork, in 2005 for his contribution to music in Ireland. Other awards include Ollamh na hÉigse (Professor of Arts) in 2005 by Comhaltas Ceoltóirí Éireann, Boston College Honorary Alumni Award for contributions to Irish music in the USA (2006), and Gradam Ceoil (Irish language television award for contribution to Irish music) in April 2011. He was appointed inaugural Chair of Culture Ireland (the statutory body for promoting Irish arts worldwide) in 2004, and reappointed in 2008.

There I was, standing in the foyer of the Irish World Academy of Music and Dance at the University of Limerick, having been invited to the opening of the Blas summer school, in 2011. I knew that it was important that I introduce myself to Professor Ó Súilleabháin – although I wasn't entirely sure why, and I was certainly unsure of how I might do it. After all, the figure standing chatting to Iarla Ó Lionárd and other Irish music notables and academics only a few feet away from me was surely one of the most important and influential musicians and teachers in the country. He has known and worked with a veritable who's-who of the very best names in Irish music and has met many heads of state and other notable figures both in Ireland and internationally. Why would he be interested in me, an unremarkable photographer? After a period of anxious self-deliberating, I decided not to risk being given the cold shoulder and made to leave. My exit was spotted by Ellen Byrne, a member of the academy staff, and I was being introduced before I knew what was happening. And then, equally as quickly, I was outlining the premise for my book to him and hearing myself asking Mícheál if he would be interested in being photographed for it. Within the week, I arrived at his home and photographed him at an upright piano painted for him by celebrated artist Henry Morgan.

A few days later, I was sitting in the foyer of the Irish World Academy of Music and Dance, waiting for a sound check to start, when I heard Mícheál enter the building. He spotted me in the corner of the large room, came over, shook my hand and asked me if I was happy with how the photography had gone. Yes, I certainly was – and I am delighted to make the acquaintance of such an ebullient, influential and supportive man as Mícheál Ó Súilleabháin. (For further information, see www.mosmusic.ie and www.irishworldacademy.ie.)

Mícheál Ó Súilleabháin with the artist Henry Morgan

Mícheál Ó Súilleabháin

A Note on Geraldine Cotter

Geraldine Cotter, from Ennis in County Clare, is a well-known teacher and performer on both the piano and the tin whistle. She is a music graduate of both University College Cork and the University of Limerick, and is currently undertaking doctoral research at the Irish World Academy of Music and Dance in the University of Limerick, where she has taught since 2002.

Geraldine has written two best-selling tutors for traditional Irish music: *Geraldine Cotter's Traditional Irish Tin Whistle Tutor* and *Seinn an Piano*, the first publication dedicated to the playing of traditional Irish music on the piano. In 2006 she published *Rogha*, a tune book with accompanying play-along CD. She also contributed to *The Companion to Irish Traditional Music* edited by Fintan Vallely and published by Cork University Press in 1999.

As well as with the group Shaskeen, she has recorded on over 20 CDs including with her brother Eamonn, Catherine McEvoy, Peadar O'Loughlin, Maeve Donnelly, Mary MacNamara, Eileen O'Brien, Tom Cussen, Tony Howley, Andrew MacNamara . . . She has performed on stage with Charlie Harris, Martin Hayes, Liz Carroll, John Carty, Gearoid O hAllmhurain, Patrick Ourceau, Joe Burke, Noel Hill, Tulla and Kilfenora Céilí Bands and Moving Cloud, and many more too numerous to mention. She spent time in the late 1970s collecting music and songs in North County Kerry for an archive that is kept in Muckross House in Killarney. She is a member of the groups Shaskeen and Ceoltoiri na Mainistreach. She performs regularly on television, radio and in concert in Ireland and abroad, and has been featured on the television documentaries *Céard an Cheoil* and *Canúintí*.

A Note from Geraldine Cotter

I grew up in Ennis in a very musical family. My mother was my first teacher and many of my family are professionally involved in music, including my brother Eamonn, a leading flute player and maker.

My piano playing style has been informed by the musicians I perform with rather than other piano players; musicians such as Sonny Murray, Peter O'Loughlin, P.J. Hayes (Martin's dad) Paddy Canny, Paddy Murphy, Junior Crehan, Bobby Casey, Paddy O'Brien. In terms of piano accompaniment without doubt my biggest influence has been Charlie Lennon, but I was also guided in this as a teenager, although not a piano player, by fiddle player Seamus Connolly.

Comhaltas Ceoltoiri Éireann was very significant for young Ennis musicians in Ennis in the 1970s, providing us with many opportunities to perform both locally and abroad.

I have played classical piano but in recent years I am better known for performing traditional music. I also have a keen interest in jazz and take every opportunity to develop that strand of my playing.'

10. The
Uilleann
Pipes

A Note on the Uilleann Pipes

The national pipes of Ireland were originally known as 'Union Pipes', but the name now used is taken from the Irish phrase *píoba uilleann*, which literally means 'elbow pipes'. This refers to the way in which the bag is filled with air, and the way that air is then forced out through the pipes – by the use of the piper's elbows, one on the bellows and the other on the bag.

Unlike the Scottish bag pipes, which were often used for marching in front of armies, the uilleann (pronounced 'ill-un') pipes have to be played sitting down. The piper is using both elbows, the pads of the fingers of both hands on the chanter (akin to a long wooden whistle – the part of the pipes that is used to play the melody) and the wrist of one hand on the keys on the regulators. If you thought patting your head while rubbing your tummy was difficult, sit down with a full set of uilleann pipes for an hour and you'll know what 'multi-tasking' really means.

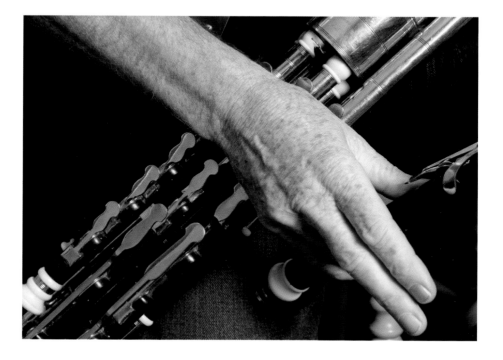

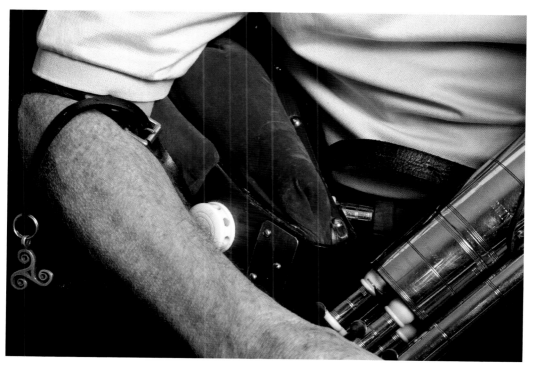

A Note on Cillian Vallely

Starting at age seven, Cillian Vallely learned the whistle and uilleann pipes from his parents Brian and Eithne at the Armagh Pipers Club, a group that for over four decades has fostered the revival of traditional music in the north of Ireland. Since leaving college, he has played professionally and has toured all over North America and Europe in addition to Japan, Hong Kong, New Zealand and Australia.

Since 1999, he has been a member of the band Lúnasa, with whom he has recorded six albums and played at many major festivals including Womad, Glastonbury, Edmonton and Winnipeg Folk Festivals, Lorient Interceltique and the Hollywood Bowl. He has also performed and toured with Riverdance, Natalie Merchant, Tim O'Brien and Mary Chapin-Carpenter in The Crossing, New York-based Whirligig, and the Celtic Jazz Collective with Lewis Nash and Peter Washington. In the past couple of years, he has worked on various collaborations between traditional and classical music, along with his brother Niall and the composer Micheál O Súilleabháin.

He has recorded on over forty albums including *Callan Bridge* with his brother Niall, *On Common Ground* with Kevin Crawford and various guest spots with Natalie Merchant, Alan Simon's Excalibur project with Fairport Convention and The Moody Blues, 'GAIA' with the Prague Philharmonic Orchestra, and singer Karan Casey. He has recently recorded on two movie soundtracks, *Irish Jam* and *The Golden Boys,* and played uilleann pipes on the BBC's *Flight of the Earls* soundtrack.

A Note on a Pipe Maker, Michael Vignoles

Uilleann pipe maker Michael Vignoles was born near Galway Bay and now lives and works in the Claddagh area of Galway city. Because his parents were both good singers who loved to play the music of Frank Sinatra, Michael was immersed in music from a very early age. While growing up, he was an avid radio listener and became a fan of such bands as Planxty, The Chieftains and The Dubliners. In particular, the sound of Liam O'Flynn's pipes made a serious impression on him.

Michael undertook a five-year apprenticeship as a fitter at the In-
stitute of the Motor Industry and around the time he qualified, he had
got himself a set of uilleann pipes that he was learning to play. When
the bellows broke on his set, he asked pipe maker Eugene Lambe from
County Clare to make him another one. But instead, Eugene gave Michael the materials and told him to make it himself. The next week, he
showed Michael how to make a reed for the chanter – with the proviso
that he should pass on the knowledge – and he continued to become
an established pipe maker in his own right.

Pipe making is a slow and painstaking business, and it can take many
weeks – if not much longer – to produce a full set of uilleann pipes.
To make a good reed for the chanter alone is a time-consuming and
painstaking process. But the rich sound of a Michael Vignoles set of
pipes makes it all worth the effort.

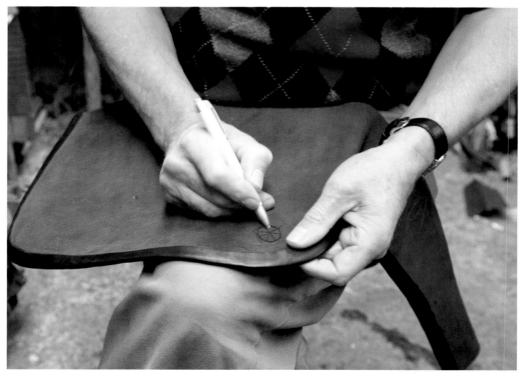

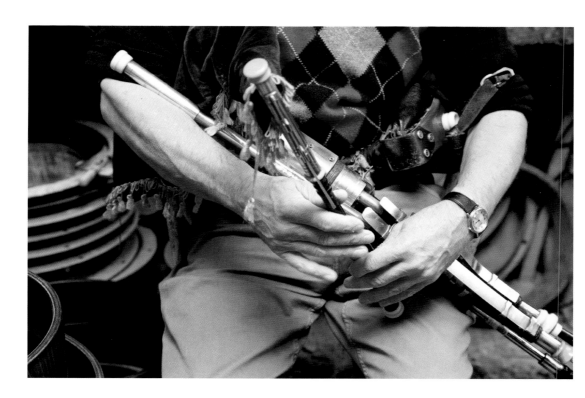

Piper James O'Grady from Luton, UK

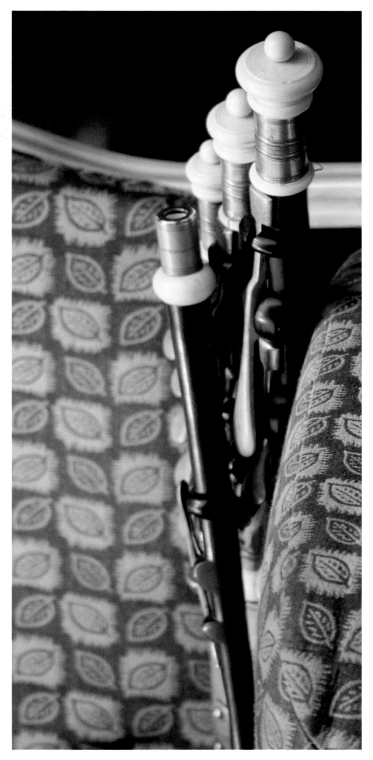

The Piper's Chair

Uilleann pipes by the late Alain Fremont

1. The Voice

A Note on the Voice

Many different styles of singing can be heard in Irish music, from the unaccompanied and ornamented sounds of the sean-nós ('old style') vocalist to powerful ballad singers and the popular vocal sounds of the contemporary singer-songwriter.

This chapter consists of images of a small, and far from comprehensive, cross-section of singers that I have been fortunate enough to photograph in the course of compiling this book.

A Note on Paul Brady

Although probably now most well known for his string of contemporary hits, Paul Brady from Strabane in County Tyrone began his long and highly successful career as a traditional Irish musician – and still performs songs from this strand of his musical life in his current live shows.

He joined an Irish folk band, The Johnstons, in 1967 and toured the UK and later the USA with them, before joining Planxty, briefly, in 1974. This led to the critically acclaimed traditional album *Andy Irvine and Paul Brady*.

Many other highly acclaimed albums and performing successes have followed and Paul Brady has garnered a reputation for being one of the best interpreters of traditional Irish songs, and one of the finest performers touring today.

A Note on Iarla Ó Lionáird

From his early days as a sean-nós singer to Afro Celt Sound System and his collaborative and solo work, Iarla Ó Lionáird, from County Cork and now living in County Kilkenny, has always ploughed his own artistic furrow. His work is very connected to the totems of traditional Irish music — sean-nós, the Irish language, traditional instrumentation — but various projects have broadened his experience and understanding in the multi-faceted nature of music.

On his third solo album, *Foxlight*, released in September 2011 just after I photographed Iarla, he delivers an 'impassioned and sublime set of personal songs, combining the twin urges to write more new material and yet also work with an intriguing set of collaborators'.

I spent a very enjoyable summer's day travelling to County Kilkenny to meet and photograph this very amiable and highly talented singer. He not only took me to visit his favourite pub – Carroll's – in Thomastown but also invited me to visit his home, to enter the inner sanctum of his private recording studio and meet his lovely family. A memorable shoot indeed.

A Note on Eleanor Shanley

Eleanor Shanley is from County Leitrim and had learned many Irish ballads when she was still very young. On leaving school, she worked for a national government-sponsored employment agency, studied drama and also sang in many sessions. This led to an introduction to Frankie Gavin and Alec Finn of De Danann, which changed her life. Within two weeks she was giving up the day job and touring Wales, Finland and Sweden.

Since then, Eleanor has sung with many well-known artists including Frankie Lane and Paul Kelly, Ronnie Drew and John Carty, amongst others, and has re-united with De Danann for recent concert tours.

I didn't know Eleanor Shanley when we hitched a lift in the minibus taking De Dannan from Hamburg airport to Toender in Denmark, for a folk festival. But her welcoming and friendly manner – and the

warm greetings every time we met backstage and at sound checks throughout that weekend – has left me feeling that we had made a friend, and hoping that we will be able to call this captivating singer a friend for a long time to come.

Eleanor Shanley with Cian Finn

A Note on John Spillane

Singer-songwriter John Spillane is a native of Cork, the county he lovingly describes as 'the centre of the universe', and which has been a huge creative influence on him. Vocally, he is quite unique with an almost sean nós-like element in his singing and he is said to have a voice 'full of honesty, commitment and sensitivity'.

He has won two Meteor awards and is one of the most accomplished songwriters in Ireland today. Among those who have covered his songs are Christy Moore, Karan Casey, Pauline Scanlon, Cathy Ryan, Sharon Shannon, Sean Keane and George Murphy, to name a few. He performs to audiences large and small everywhere.

The first thing I noticed about John Spillane, when I first met him several years ago, was his dry quirky humour. It can be found not only in his song lyrics – such as 'Johnny Don't go to Ballincollig' (a town in County Cork) – but also in his between-songs banter with an audience – 'it's going well so far; fair play to me' and 'this next song will be sung not in my own language, but in the language of the oppressor' (referring to English) and 'welcome to The Hit Factory' (referring to himself).

He is a good-natured, easy-going man who committed himself to my photography for this book with his inherent sense of fun — and I hope the resulting photographs show it. I would like to think I'll photograph him again soon, but I can almost hear him respond in his droll, Cork accent, 'dream on Stephen, dream on'.

A Note on Karan Casey

Karan Casey has long been regarded as one of the most innovative, provocative and imitated voices in Irish traditional and folk music. Her career has spanned twenty years – from the early days as a jazz performer in George's Bistro in Dublin, to her heady days in New York with the band Solas – and she has sold over half a million albums.

Karan has won awards for 'Best Folk Album' and 'Best Folk Female' from *Irish Music Magazine* and been nominated for the BBC Folk Awards and the Danish Grammys, and was a key member of Paul Winter's Grammy-award winning *Celtic Solstice*. She has appeared at many prestigious venues, including the Kennedy Centre (Washington, DC), New York's Symphony Space, Nashville's Grand Ole Opry, the Hollywood Bowl, Dublin's National Concert Hall, the Cathedral of St John the Divine, the Glasgow Royal Concert Hall and many others. She has also made many TV and radio appearances on both sides of the Atlantic.

A Note on Michelle Lally

Michelle Lally was born in County Galway and sings with Frankie Gavin's band The New De Dannan. Michelle has been described as 'a powerful singer whose renditions of contemporary easy listening Irish music are impossible to resist with the gentle charm of her immediately identifiable pure tone.'

Michelle's debut album, *If This Be Love*, features songs by some of Ireland's leading songwriters such as Jimmy MacCarthy, Mick Hanly and John Spillane. She has been described by Jimmy MacCarthy as having 'a voice that lingers in the mind's ear, when the enchanted listening is done', and Mick Hanly has said her voice is 'truly beautiful and beautifully true'.

While photographing at the sound check for a recent performance in County Limerick, I chatted to Michelle about hearing her rendition of the Edith Piaf song 'If You Love Me' and asked if she would be singing it that night. My evening was complete when not only did Michelle sing it, beautifully, but also dedicated the song . . . to me.

A Note on Máire Ní Chéileachair

Máire Ní Chéileachair is widely regarded as one of the finest singers in the sean-nós tradition. I was fortunate enough to photograph her at the Masters of Tradition concerts in Bantry, West Cork.

12. The Whistle

A Note on the Whistle

Tin-whistle, penny whistle, flageolet or just plain 'whistle' – call it what you will – but this is one of the oldest, simplest and most popular instruments in Irish traditional music. It generally consists of a short tube with six holes and a mouthpiece, sometimes called a 'fipple'. The original commercially produced 'tin whistles' – made by Robert Clarke in the UK from 1840 to 1882 – were sold for a penny each, hence the name 'Penny Whistle', although some historians say that a penny was also the price paid to early buskers playing the whistles on the streets.

Whistles are no longer made of tin, the most common material being brass or nickel plating – they are also made in varying forms of plastics and other metals – but they can still be bought for less than half the price of a music download, making them extremely popular with children, and for teaching music in schools. The more experienced players will prefer to buy high-end or hand-made whistles, and whistle makers have long waiting lists for instruments that can cost well into three figures.

Whistles come in many different musical 'keys' – one of the most popular being the key of D, which can also play the notes in the G scale, the two most common keys used in traditional Irish music.

Although it's a very simple construction and often cheap to buy, the whistle is far from easy to play well. I have heard children in the street blowing a tuneless shrill out a cheap brass *feadóg* (the Irish word for whistle) and a similar whistle in the mouth and hands of skilled players making wonderful, heart-wrenching sounds that seem impossible to produce on such a simple instrument.

A Note on the Low Whistle

The low whistle is a longer, wider instrument than the standard whistle and is usually pitched an octave lower – for example, 'the low D' whistle. This gives it a deeper and more mellow tone and to my ear it is closer to the sound of a wooden flute than a whistle. Because of the size and wider spacings of the holes in the body, the low whistle is usually played by covering the holes with the pads of the fingers after the first knuckle, and not with the tips of the fingers, as the higher pitched, shorter whistle would be played.

This technique is very similar to that used by pipers on the 'chanter' – and many uilleann pipers also choose to play the low whistle.

Kevin Crawford of Lúnasa playing the low whistle

Cillian Vallely of Lúnasa playing the low whistle

A Note on Whistle Player Mary Bergin

Mary Bergin is recognised as one of the world's greatest players and teachers of the tin whistle. And, in my view, she is one of the nicest and most helpful people in traditional music. Unusally, Mary plays the whistle left-handed with the right hand covering the upper tone holes, unlike most whistle players who play with the left hand on top.

Mary was born in Shankill, County Dublin in 1949 and began learning to play the whistle when she was nine years old. At the age of nineteen, she won the All Ireland tin whistle championship and has made two of the most critically aclaimed recordings of solo tin whistle playing – *Feadóga Stáin* (1979) and *Feadóga Stáin 2* (1993) – which did a great deal to popularise the playing of traditional Irish music on the whistle. These recording were hailed as 'outstanding and unequalled' by Fintan Vallely and Charlie Piggott in their 1998 book *Blooming Meadows*.

Mary has lived in Spiddal in County Galway since the 1970s and that was where I photographed her – and sampled her excellent coffee – at her lovely home. She is currently a member of the group Dordán, who perform Irish traditional music and Baroque music.

As well as her own re-cording successes, her play-ing with many famous artists and bands – including Noel Hill and De Dannan – Mary Bergin has taught many hun-dreds of people to play the whistle, not only in Ireland but also across Europe and the USA.

Paul Brady playing a whistle

Piper James O'Grady playing a low whistle

Lúnasa playing low whistles

13. Playing Live

A Note on Playing Live

Irish traditional music is meant to be played and heard live. Whether it's at home, in a pub session, in a small parish hall, a larger theatre or even at a major festival with an audience of thousands – nothing compares to watching and listening while the fiddles, flutes, pipes, accordions and bodhráns come alive in the hands of talented musicians.

A fascinating thing, I've noticed, about Irish traditional music is that it is a reasonably small and interchangeable society. Although many musicians are permanent members of a particular group or band (perhaps even more than one), it is not uncommon for those members to come together in other permutations, perhaps for a pub session or a small gig when they are not playing with their main band.

Because of that, and because they frequently meet up at the same concerts or festivals, standing backstage at an Irish music concert, and

listening to the various conversations, can feel a bit like having gate-crashed a large family reunion: 'I heard that you did a great show in Dublin'; 'Will you be at Milwaukee this year?'; 'Great news about Billy getting that record deal, wasn't it?' and so on. There is often a wonderfully friendly atmosphere around such events and it can be a great boost to the psyche just to stand there and let it rub off on you.

The bands photographed live for this book included De Dannan, Lúnasa, Frankie Gavin (with his band The New De Dannan), The Dubliners and the duo Martin Hayes and Dennis Cahill. There were also groupings of musicians who play in different bands – or who may be best known as solo performers – playing together at special events, including the Blas International Summer School of Irish Traditional Music and Dance at the University of Limerick or the Masters of Tradition concerts held annually in Bantry, West Cork.

John Carty and Dónal Lunny rehearsing

Kevin Crawford, Tony Linnane and Mick Conneely

Lúnasa playing live at Toender Folk Festival

A Note on Live Music Photography

Live music photography can be very challenging – light levels are often lower than desirable for a usable exposure, leaving shutter speeds too slow to crisply capture the action and making focusing difficult. Plus, if like me you're a fan of the music, it's easy to become distracted from the job at hand because you're too busy listening.

There is an unwritten 'code' amongst the more experienced music photographers, which is good to see put into practice no matter where I may be photographing. Firstly, professional music photographers will not use flash guns for two reasons: it distracts the musicians and effectively kills the vivid colours and atmosphere produced by good stage lighting. Standing in front of the paying audience is another 'no-no', and music photographers often find themselves sitting on the floor or working from the side of the stage – or even sitting on small, uncomfortable seats built into the barrier between the stage and the audience at larger gigs.

Also, it's not appropriate to fire the shutter during the quieter moments of a performance, as a loud shutter click can be heard over the music in small venues – and many 'great shots' go uncaptured by those of us who choose to abide by that particular unwritten rule. Walking in front of another photographer while they are aiming their camera towards the stage is probably the worst offence that can be committed, and it's not unusual to see photographers laden down with cameras and long zoom lenses bending forwards at the waist and doing the strange 'snapper-shuffle' (as I like to call it) as they move around in front of the stage.

Challenges aside, I feel completely in my element when I get up close with my camera to a talented musician or band playing live. I have learned to try to wait for the 'right moment' before pressing the shutter – such as when a singer leans away from the microphone – and experience has taught me to know when the stage lighting is too low or too red or too soft to show the subject clearly. Sometimes I just fire away regardless of all my experience, buoyed up by the adrenaline coursing through me, and the resulting images – if worth keeping – are a product of good luck rather than good photography. But sometimes, just sometimes, I calm down and put my learning into practice – and it all comes together in a photograph worthy of publication.

Martin Hayes and Dennis Cahill

Frankie Gavin's band The New De Danaan

The Dubliners at Toender Folk Festtival

Sandra Joyce and Mícheál Ó Súilleabháin

Johnny 'Ringo' McDonagh and others at Toender Folk Festival

Riches of Clare concert in Ennis, County Clare

Dónal Lunny, John Carty and Séamus Begley

De Danaan at Toender Folk Festival

Finale at Toender Folk Festival with Eamonn Campbell centre

A Note on Stephen Power

Stephen Power is an extraordinary photographer who also has a huge passion for music. When the idea for this book first came to him, and I am sure it had been formulating in his mind for some time, it was to fulfil not only his love for photography, but also to tap into his huge knowledge about the music industry, musicians and their instruments. *Traditional Notes* just had to be done.

Stephen has been a photographer long before I knew him (he admits to 28 years) and has been associated with the music industry both in the UK and Ireland for even longer, including owning a music shop for a spell in Adare, County Limerick. During this time he also organised musical events, and played the bouzouki in traditional music sessions.

From beginning to end, it has been a wonderful experience to have been involved in the creation of this book. At times, I remember thinking, 'Is this really happening?' We did whatever it took to get to where the next photograph was to be taken. We drove many hundreds of kilometres around Ireland – staying in hotels and B&Bs, exploring new parts of the country, getting lost at times, but always finding our way in the end. Stephen even arranged for us to fly to Denmark to attend a folk music festival, and at very short notice. His drive and creativity is obvious when he wants to get the job done!

An amazing part of this photographic journey was being invited into people's homes, and being made to feel very welcome. These were well known musicians and instrument makers whom Stephen was asking to take time from their busy schedules to sit for photographs, and to discuss their involvement in the music industry. This is, I feel, where he truly came into his own. His ease at getting people to do what was needed to create a good photograph was extraordinary. It was interesting to watch the expressions change on their faces, and their questions change from 'what is this about?' to 'well, what can I do to help you?'

It was not hard to see why this was happening, as from the moment he started to discuss the book his passion for the subject, and his determination to get it just right, were obvious. He could take a long time getting the right photograph – or the photograph right – and he often did. The right photograph may not have been evident immediately, but with patience – and experience – it would evolve as the shoot progressed. Also, it frequently occurred that a 'standard' photographic shoot turned into several hours of great company with food and drink being provided along with great stories and laughter. We even had a dog play the piano for us on one occasion.

I gained many insights into various aspects of professional photography during the time it took to complete this book. But the biggest insight was watching Stephen work – seeing how he created the more than 5,000 photographs to choose from for this book, and understanding what it took for him to be satisfied that he had done it well.

Marjorie Brickley
September 2011